Breaking Through by Grace

Other Books in the Zonderkidz Biography Series

Gifted Hands: The Ben Carson Story
Man on a Mission: The Tim Tebow Story
Toward the Goal: The Kaká Story

Breaking Through by Grace

the
Bono
Story

Kim Washburn

ZONDERVAN.com/
AUTHORTRACKER
follow your favorite authors

*For the indispensable K.K. and Andrew,
my most essential collaborator.*

ZONDERKIDZ

Breaking Through by Grace: The Bono Story
Copyright © 2010 by Kim Washburn

This title is also available as a Zondervan ebook.
Visit www.zondervan.com/ebooks.

Requests for information should be addressed to:
Zonderkidz, Grand Rapids, Michigan 49530

Library of Congress Cataloging-in-Publication Data

Washburn, Kim, 1970–
    Breaking through by grace : the Bono story / by Kim Washburn.
        p. cm. – (Zonderkidz biography)
        ISBN 978-0-310-72123-9 (softcover)
        1. Bono, 1960– –Juvenile literature. 2. Rock musicians—Biography—Juvenile
    literature. 3. Christian biography. I. Title.
    ML3930.B592W37 2010
    782.42166092—dc22
    [B]   2010025815

All Scripture quotations, unless otherwise indicated, are taken from the Holy Bible,
New International Version®, NIV®. Copyright © 1973, 1978, 1984 by Biblica, Inc.™ Used
by permission of Zondervan. All rights reserved worldwide.

Any Internet addresses (websites, blogs, etc.) and telephone numbers printed in this
book are offered as a resource. They are not intended in any way to be or imply an
endorsement by Zondervan, nor does Zondervan vouch for the content of these sites
and numbers for the life of this book.

Zonderkidz is a trademark of Zondervan.

Art direction: Cindy Davis
Cover design: Kris Nelson
Cover photo: AP Photo/Manu Fernandez
Interior design: Ben Fetterley, Greg Johnson/Textbook Perfect

Printed in the United States of America

10 11 12 13 14 15 /DCI/ 10 9 8 7 6 5 4 3 2 1

Contents

Chapter 1

When Love Storms a Stadium

The Roar of the Stadium

No matter who wins or loses this football game, the crowd is going to cry.

It has been five months since September 11, 2001, when a terrorist attack on the United States took thousands of lives by hijacking four airplanes and flying them into buildings.

America is still struggling to get off her knees. Now a rock band from Ireland is about to help her up.

This rock band, U2, had been inspiring audiences all over the world for more than twenty years. And on this night, February 3, 2002, they set up their heart-shaped stage in the biggest arena America had to offer: halftime at the Super Bowl.

In the darkness of the arena, energy surges through the audience like a lightning storm. U2's powerful song

"Beautiful Day" has thundered through the stadium and faded out. Seventy thousand voices are screaming their support.

Then, unexpectedly, a gigantic screen, as long as the stage and as high as the stadium, rises behind the band. The glowing white words "September 11th, 2001" scroll to the sky, followed by the name of each person who died in the terrorist attacks that day.

Later Bono, the lead singer of the band, would admit, "I [couldn't] look at the names. If I looked at the names, I wouldn't be able to sing." So he faces the crowd, his voice burning through the emotion of the night as he sings a haunting lullaby.

Sleep. Sleep tonight. And may your dreams be realized ...

Then a cascade of notes from the electric guitar signals the beginning of a new song. The drums and the bass join in to drive the beat.

Muffled by the boom of the sound system and the cheers of the crowd, Bono, the biggest rock star in the world, utters a prayer from Psalm 51:15: "O Lord, open my lips, and my mouth shall show forth your praise."

As the procession of names floats past, Bono calls out "America!" Cheers explode from the stadium, and Bono runs around the entire heart-shaped stage that embraces the crowd. And then he takes the microphone and sings U2's anthem of love and hope, "Where the Streets Have No Name."

The band could play all night and the song would feel too short. When the screen falls to the ground, Bono makes the shape of a heart on his chest with his hands.

Bono performs during halftime of Super Bowl XXXVI in New Orleans, Louisiana, on February 3, 2002.

Jeff Haynes/AFP/Getty Images

Then the singer opens his jacket and reveals that the fabric of the liner is an American flag. The music surrenders to the shouts of the frenzied crowd. Tears stream down the cheeks of everyone in the stadium.

Bono has sung a love song to the wounded hearts of Americans.

The Quiet of the Back Room

Two days before the Super Bowl, far away from huge stages and cheering crowds, Bono had been composing a different kind of love song.

At midnight in New York City, he slipped into a restaurant and made his way to the back room. A diverse group of decision makers, strategists, financial planners, church leaders, and generous donors were huddled around tables. Together they wanted to come up with serious, practical ways to end extreme poverty. Extreme poverty occurs when a person cannot pay for food, water, shelter, clothing, or health care. Today, there are almost one and a half billion people living in these conditions — many of them in South Asia and Africa. Ending extreme poverty in the world would take lots of fresh ideas, money, commitment, and prayer. But that was why this group had gathered: they wanted to change the world.

Bono had not come here to make music. He was here to make a difference.

"When you sing," Bono explained, "you make people [open] to change in their lives. You make yourself [open] to change in your life. But in the end, you've got to become the change you want to see in the world. I'm actually not a very good example of that — I'm too selfish, and the right to be ridiculous is something I hold too dear — but still, I know it's true."[1]

This gathering of people fighting to end poverty was part of the World Economic Forum, which is an organization that seeks to improve the lives of ordinary people all around the world. This wasn't exactly the place you'd go to find a rock star! But Bono's heart had been moved by the desperately poor, the people that Jesus called the "least of these." When Bono read the Bible, he found over two thousand verses about poverty. Jesus cared about the poor, and he reached out to the "untouchables" of his age. "It couldn't be more [obvious]," Bono said, "that this is on God's mind, that this is Jesus' point of view."[2]

And so Bono goes into unexpected places to work with unexpected people. He follows his heart and uses his powerful gift of communication with politicians and preachers, presidents, and popes.

It's unusual for a rock star—especially a rock star as well-known as Bono—to spend time working for others. "I know how absurd it is to have a rock star talk about the World Health Organization or debt relief or ... AIDS in Africa," he said.[3] But he also knows that when he talks, people listen.

This night in New York City, Bono joined a serious discussion. As a team they would learn from experts, try to understand the issues and the problems, and come up with practical ways to change the world for the desperately poor. The man who sang in front of millions of cheering fans wanted to lend his voice to those who had none.

As a young man, Bono's heart had simply led him to music. But once he was in a band, working with friends to create music that moved him, love came into the room, made itself comfortable, and decided to make some changes. Now love wanted him to move mountains.

Before love took over, though, rage had its day for Bono.

Chapter 2

Steinvic von Huyseman Takes on the Tears

A House, Not a Home

Before the rock star, before the voice, before the music, before the famous name, Bono was Paul David Hewson. He was born on May 10, 1960—the second son of Bob and Iris Hewson.

At the time Ireland, his proud and beloved country, was engaging in a civil war. Catholics and Protestants raged over their differences. They drew battle lines based on the differences in what they believed. The violence went on for a long time, and before it was over more than 3,000 people had died. This time in Ireland's history is called "The Troubles."

Because the two groups of people were so suspicious of each other, they lived in separate neighborhoods and attended separate schools in separate parts of the city.

Ireland was boiling. "I grew up in what you would call a lower-middle-class neighborhood," Bono said. "[It was] a nice street and good people. And, yet, if I'm honest, a sense that violence was around the corner."[4]

To this day, Bono is saddened that religion had been the cause of so much pain and violence. "We've seen [religious differences] tear our country in two," he said. "You hold onto religion ... rules, regulations, traditions. I think what God is interested in is people's hearts."[5]

Bono's parents, Iris and Bob, fell in love and got married under highly unusual circumstances, since Bob was Catholic and Iris was Protestant. Their love for each other mattered more than the differences in the way they practiced their faith, and they didn't take sides in the Troubles that were tearing Ireland apart. Even at a young age, Bono understood that their family's lack of extreme sides in the religion wars made them different in their neighborhood.

Bono attended a Protestant primary school called the Ink Bottle. Occasionally, when the headmaster looked the other way, Bono and the other students would kick a ball over the fence that followed along the river and chase after it. "It has very good memories for me, that school," Bono once said with a laugh.[6]

But the next school Bono attended, St. Patrick's Cathedral Choir School, didn't hold the same affection for him. "I spent a year at St. Patrick's, not being happy, and basically they asked me to leave," he admitted.[7]

In 1972, Bono moved to a different school. This one was two bus rides away through Dublin's City Centre.

The school, Mount Temple Comprehensive School, was Ireland's first coed, nondenominational high school. A school that didn't segregate between Catholics and Protestants was a groundbreaking idea in a society so deeply rooted in religious turmoil. Bono, however, had grown up in a nondenominational home. He settled in just fine.

Bono was confident, popular, and full of mischief and fun. But more than anything else he was drawn to music. "I've always heard kind of melodies in my head," said Bono, remembering those early days. "I remember standing under a piano at my grandmother's house, when the keys of the piano were higher than my head. [I remember] pressing down on the keys, and then hearing one note and ... looking for another one to follow it."[8]

Like a puzzle to be solved and a story to be told, the melodies in Bono's head had to be sung. Bono would hear a note and want to—*have to*—find the next in the sequence. Whether he inherited a musical gene from his opera-loving father or received it as a gift from God, Bono had a heart for music and a mind for melody.

In 1974, the Hewsons' world suddenly fell apart. At the funeral of her own father, Bono's mom, Iris, suffered a massive brain hemorrhage. Bono was only fourteen years old, and his older brother, Norman, was twenty-one. Their mother's abrupt and all-too-sudden death left a grieving family to clumsily, painfully feel their way through the darkness. "Our mother was gone, the beautiful Iris ... I felt abandoned, afraid," said Bono about this difficult time. "I guess fear converts to anger pretty quickly."[9]

The rooms in the house had become crowded with emotion that none of them quite knew how to deal with. "It became a house of men," Bono explained. "And three, it turns out, quite macho men—and all that goes with that. The aggression thing is something I'm still working at."[10]

Ultimately, Bono's family was not able to rally to one another. Bono's uncommunicative father tried to keep the family together, but instead of connecting, the three men clashed. Aunts tried to step in, but fourteen-year-old Bono wasn't open to any warmth. His brother, Norman, was dealing with his own sorrow. "Both of us admitted that we were just angry at each other because we didn't know how to grieve, you see ... Because my mother was never mentioned."[11]

Bono's father, Bob, believed that "to dream is to be disappointed." This went against everything Bono knew in his heart to be true.[12] Bono knew that he had to pursue his dreams in spite of the difficult circumstances he was growing up in. He has spent his entire life being driven by big ideas and big dreams.

Belonging in the Village

Even though anger and conflict had taken over Bono's relationship with his family, his connections with his friends were easy and secure. He hung out with a group of boys who referred to themselves as "Lypton Village."

They were a tight gang of creative dreamers. Relying on each other, they found peace, escape, and harmony.

Because of his friends, Bono became more and more aware of his dependence on other people. At first he saw this dependence as a weakness, but eventually he came to understand an important truth. "The blessing of your weakness is it forces you into friendships," Bono said. "The things that you lack, you look for in others."[13]

These Lypton Village friends had a special ritual: they gave each other unique nicknames. These new names tied the close friends tighter. Bono had a number of these names. First, his friends called him "Steinvic von Huyseman." This was soon shortened to "Huyseman" and later modified to "Houseman." Shortly after that, the name changed altogether and became "Bon Murray." This name morphed into "Bono Vox of O'Connell Street," which was abbreviated into "Bono Vox" and finally cut to "Bono." "The only person who ever called me Paul was my father," Bono said later, "so I always associate [that name] with doing something wrong."[14] The shortened name stuck, and so did the friendships.

The Lypton Village gang—Bono, Gavin Friday, and Guggi—became lifelong friends. They were bonded by shared history and senses of humor. Inspired, imaginative, and often ridiculous, they colored the world with laughter. "We'd put on performances in the City Centre of Dublin," Bono recalled. "I'd get on the bus with a stepladder and an electric drill. Humor became our weapon. I just [stood] there, quiet—with the drill in my hand."[15]

Bono could be as serious as a professor, but his history of pranks and ridiculous jokes was long and proud. "Once my mates came to wrap my car in tissue paper—the entire car—with dozens and dozens of eggs. [They] turned it into papier-mâché, [sealing] it like in a cocoon of tissue and eggs. And when I woke up, they were firing eggs at me. Only problem was my father woke up!"[16]

While there were plenty of wacky shenanigans, the friendships proved serious and steadfast.

"I remember that whenever it was Guggi's birthday, which is three days after mine," said Bono, "whatever he got from his family, or whatever [he got] in cash, he would split with me fifty-fifty. And he ... taught me one of the fundamentals, which is about sharing.... That's what I remember about birthdays. I remember Guggi's birthday."[17]

Even apart from the Lypton Village friends, when Bono was growing up he spent a lot of time with Guggi's family. Guggi's dad quoted Scripture in a way that made the boys snicker a bit—but at the same time they paid attention. "His father was like a creature from the Old Testament," Bono remembered. "He spoke constantly of the Scriptures."[18] The Bible, with its rich language and wisdom, started to seep in.

If God was whispering, Bono's heart was responding. "I prayed more outside of the church than inside. It gets back to the songs I was listening to: to me, they were prayers. 'How many roads must a man walk down?'—that wasn't a rhetorical question to me. It was addressed to God. It's a question I wanted to know the answer to, and I'm wondering, who do I ask that to? I'm not gonna ask a schoolteacher."[19]

Bono had already walked some roads—out of tragedy and conflict, through dependence and creativity, toward God. But his journey was just getting started.

Chapter 3

The Drum Kit Saves the Boy

Answering the Call

Before there were guitars and drum sets in the rock star's life, Bono just had whispers of melodies in his head. Maybe he could plunk out a few notes on a piano or pluck his brother's guitar. Maybe he could even piece together an expressive verse with a melody. But more often Bono would want to say something and have no fitting way to express it.

Then, in the fall of 1976, a notice was posted by a fourteen-year-old drummer named Larry Mullen on the bulletin board at the Mount Temple Comprehensive School. Larry was looking to start a band.

"You have to go," one of Bono's friends said. He got Bono on the back of his motorcycle and together they sped to 60 Rosemount Avenue. Once there, Bono greeted Larry and followed him inside to the "studio"—the kitchen. Little did Bono know that one day, he and Larry would be the lead singer and the drummer of one of the biggest bands in the world.

"Larry is in this tiny kitchen, and he's got his drum kit set up," Bono recalled. "And there are a few other boys. There's Dave Evans—a kinda brainy-looking kid—who's fifteen. And his brother Dik—even brainier-looking—who's built his own guitar."[20]

They were joined by another teenager named Adam Clayton, who, Bono said, "was the oldest, and he looked the most professional. He arrived with a bass guitar and a bass amp, and he looked incredible."[21]

When Bono took in the scene, excitement coursed through him like electricity running through a wire. "Larry starts playing the [drums]," he remembered. "It's an amazing sound, just hit the cymbal. [Dave] hit a guitar chord which I'd never heard on electric guitar."[22]

This was the calling that Bono's heart and mind had been waiting for without even knowing it. To develop melodies, to work together with friends on songs that had always moved him, to communicate through music—for Bono it was "the open road." His dreams just got a whole lot bigger.

Their first rehearsal made an impression on people in the neighborhood just as much as on Bono. "Kids started coming from all around the place—all girls," Bono recalled. "They know that Larry lives there. They're ... screaming; they're ... climbing up the door. [Larry] was completely used to this, we discovered," Bono laughs.[23]

In the world of rock-and-roll music, this enthusiasm from fans was a good sign. Their band just might have a future.

The experience of making music was fun, exciting, and new. But to Bono it meant even more than that. "What's interesting is in the months leading up to this, I was probably at the lowest [point] in my life," Bono would say later. "I was feeling just teenage angst. I didn't know if I wanted to continue living—that kind of despair. I was praying to a God I didn't know was listening."[24]

Inspired Collaborations

After a few weeks of rehearsing, the band of Bono, Larry, Adam, and brothers Dave and Dik decided to name themselves "Feedback." This name came at least partly from the shrill sound coming back through the amplifier when they played. At first, Feedback just played songs they already knew from the radio or records. At least they knew how those songs were *supposed* to sound. Unfortunately, the versions Feedback played didn't sound much like them.

At this point Feedback had much more desire than ability.

Plus, Adam had been keeping a secret. "He had all the musician talk," Bono said. "He looked funky, he acted funky. We didn't realize at the time he couldn't play a note!" he laughed. "And so big was his bluff that we looked pretty much everywhere else to why we were sounding so [bad]. Him!"[25]

But with practice and experience, everybody's technique and ability to play their instruments gradually grew stronger. It helped, too, that the band scrapped the idea of playing other people's music. They found it easier to perform their *own* songs. Finally, Bono had the perfect place for his own melodies.

"If you wake up in the morning with a melody in your head, as I do," he explained, "it's all about how [you] take [that melody] out of your head and put it into music. Had I not got [Dave] close by, who [is] an extraordinarily gifted, complex musician, I would be hopeless. Had I not got Larry and Adam, these melodies would not be grounded."[26]

As the group's music found its groove, so did their friendships. "I'd say Larry and I were pretty close friends," Bono said. When the band was on tour, they usually shared a room. They thought of themselves as an odd couple. Larry was always very clean and organized. He would even bring his own sleeping bag to hotels because he was worried that the bed sheets were dirty. Bono, however, was the opposite. He didn't mind if there were clothes on the floor or dirty sheets on the bed.[27]

Odd couple or not, Larry and Bono shared a friendship that came from both tragedy and loyalty. They had both lost their mothers while they were still teenagers. Bono was only fourteen when his mother passed away, and Larry was sixteen. After their mothers died, both boys were raised by very strict fathers.[28] This shared experience helped the outgoing Bono and the reserved Larry to bond both as bandmates and friends.

But Larry wasn't the only friend Bono made in Feedback. He also became close to Dave Evans, who played the electric guitar. Before too much time had gone by, Bono had nicknamed Dave "The Edge." Not only did the two young men share a love for simple, single names, they shared a sense of humor. Unlike with some other bands, the uncommon circus life on a stage helped to bond the band instead of tearing them apart.

Within thirty days of climbing on the back of the motorcycle to play music in a kitchen, Bono made another move, just as bold as joining a band. He asked out a girl he knew from school, Alison Stewart (or Ali for short). "It was a good month," he grinned. "I met the most extraordinary woman, and I couldn't let her go. At the heart of my relationship is a great friendship."[29] Six years later, on August 21, 1982, Bono and Ali were married in Dublin.

The music—its power, its possibilities, its messages, its melodies—sprung laughter and loyalties, big ideas and big dreams. "That's ... the key to all the important doors in my life," Bono explained, "whether it's the band, or whether it's my marriage, or whether it's the community that I still live in. It's almost like the two sorts of sacraments are music and friendship."[30]

The Open Road

When Bono was young and still in school, he earned some extra spending money by working at a gas station. While he pumped gas, his thoughts would drift back to

Ebet Roberts/Redferns/Getty Images

Bono and his wife, Ali Hewson, backstage at the US Festival at San Bernardino.

the band and their practice sessions. Those rehearsals meant everything to Bono. The clang of a cymbal or the riff of an electric guitar moved him in ways he could hardly express.[31]

But how far could passion and enthusiasm really take a band of teenagers?

"Our talents weren't really the obvious ones that you need for this particular journey," Bono admitted. "But it turned out we had other [talents], which were maybe more important." There was something original about the group's point of view, even if they didn't always express it very well. And they were relentless.[32]

Even if the group didn't have much experience or very good musical technique, the band members could gain both of those things. After endless hours of playing, practices, run-throughs, and rehearsals, they improved. But some parts of making music couldn't be learned, bought, copied, or faked. They either had it — an indescribable quality that people connect with — or they didn't. According to audiences, they had it.

"Sparks go off when we play in a room," Bono said frankly. "There's a kind of magic. I remember bands that were much better than us at the time. Technically they looked better. We used to have an expression. We used to say, 'They have everything, but *it*.' We had nothing, but *it*."[33]

Usually, Feedback just performed in their school gym. But in 1978 they got the chance to show their raw promise to a larger audience. On St. Patrick's Day that year they won a talent show in Limerick, Ireland, and walked away with 500 pounds (about $750) and studio access to record a demo for CBS Ireland. Winning this contest confirmed what Feedback had already suspected. They had "it."

Three days later Dik Evans, Edge's brother, decided that it was time for him to leave the band and move on to other activities. He played his last gig with the band, and then Bono, Edge, Larry, and Adam decided to make one more change. Without Dik they weren't really Feedback anymore. The band needed a new name.

After playing around with different ideas, an album cover designer named Steven Averill came up with the name U2. The band agreed. Bono admitted later he didn't always like it. Did it refer to a submarine, a spy plane, or a peace movement? "It's just I never thought about it as in ... 'you too,'" he smiled. "I really didn't, but that's me."[34]

Regardless of Bono's misgivings, the name was fixed. Bono, Larry, Adam, and Edge would be U2 as they wrote and performed hundreds of songs on thirteen albums over the next three decades.

But before all the albums and concerts, U2 had to follow the same difficult road that every band must walk when it starts out. They recorded their first demo tape, gave their first interview in *Hot Press*, and played their biggest gig for a whopping fifty pounds (about seventy-five dollars).

Bono thought he knew a way to help get the band recognized outside of Ireland, but first he needed some extra money. Fifty pounds split between four band members didn't go very far! Bono borrowed money and he went to London. As long as the money lasted, he visited record companies and music magazines around the city to drop off tapes that U2 had recorded.

About the same time, the band played extra concerts at home in Ireland. Usually they played in clubs in the evenings, but they decided to take a break from the nighttime concerts. Instead, U2 gave six afternoon concerts in Dublin. Their audience grew almost instantly. Young music fans loved the live U2 summer concerts.

And U2 loved their home crowd. And so began a long Irish romance.

At the end of 1979, the band released their first single, "Three." They watched it rise on the Irish charts. As it rose, they were invited to film a concert for television in Cork Opera House, the biggest concert hall in Ireland.

Bono's music tour was also paying off in London. All of a sudden Britain was calling. Bono, Larry, Adam, and Edge borrowed 3,000 pounds (about $4,500) from their families and friends. They packed their suitcases (and Larry's sleeping bag) and headed across the water to England. It was the first time the band had ever played a show outside of Ireland, and they spent two weeks performing in the clubs there.

Sparks were going off, and U2's audiences were becoming huge fans, following the band wherever they were playing. Plus, the band members were becoming skilled musicians. The music they made was matching their passion. Even though the band was still just earning fifty pounds for every concert they played, Bono felt richer than ever.

"Wherever I feel more myself, wherever I feel the inspiration is, I want to be," Bono said. "So, in my case, being in a band, I feel completely free."[35]

Chapter 4

The Back Door to Heaven

When Love Takes Over

The lyrics, the beat, and the hard-driving sound of the band cleared out Bono's heart—a heart that had been crowded with bitterness and anger—and opened it up to love. It grounded him in his relationships and channeled his raging energy into writing music and performing on stage. All of the burning emotions and questions that had been bottled up in his heart could now flow out in full expression. "Rock 'n' roll is not about playing the right notes," Bono said. "It's about a feeling inside you that you want to get out."[36]

The music U2 was making wasn't just aimless musings or random reflections. For Bono, the songs were actually prayers. He found himself in music that tried to understand and describe humanity's relationship with God, whether that was a relationship of anger or of praise.[37]

The music helped Bono process the relationship he had with God. As he explored God's unfailing love, he wrestled with loving others and loving the world. Bono was hesitant to call himself a Christian. "[I struggle] to approach that word," he admitted. "I don't feel worthy to use the word 'Christian' because I know too much about myself. I'd be ... the one who'd just stick my hand out to grab at the hem of [Jesus'] robe," Bono said.[38]

As he explored the wisdom of the Scriptures, Bono found a Christian group in Dublin that fed him spiritually as well. The group's name was Shalom, which means peace. Shalom had no ties to a specific church. They weren't Catholic or Protestant. The group was saddened and angry about the Troubles between the two churches, and they looked for a different idea. They said God was above church divisions. Bono, along with Larry and Edge, found harmony and strength in the community of believers.

"People who had cash shared it. They were passionate, and they were funny, and they seemed to have no material desires," said Bono. "Their teaching of the Scriptures reminded me of those people whom I'd heard as a youngster with Guggi."[39]

Shalom showed how love could open people up. They lived as a community, dependent on each other for material things and dependent on God for his grace.

"At that time ... I lived with no possessions," Bono explained. "We were part of a community. Everyone helped each other out, sharing what little money we had. It was like a church that was really committed to changing the world, really. Not in a gigantic way but in small ways: individual by individual."[40]

Bono lived simply and strictly. He learned more about the Bible and other Christian writings. He listened as a respected leader of the Shalom community opened up the Bible and answered some of life's many questions.

For several years, Bono went to listen to this leader's sermons every few days. He learned a great deal about the Bible, coming to understand that the teachings of Christ were more than just words. They held the greatest Truth the world has ever known.[41] Excited about God and excited about the future, Bono told the leader that when the band made it big, they would be able to help the community financially.

But the leader's reaction took him by surprise. He just looked at Bono and laughed. Bono was hurt and confused, and asked what was wrong. "I wouldn't want money earned that way," said the leader.

Bono didn't understand. "What do you mean by that?" he asked.

The leader explained that even though he knew Bono, Larry, and Edge were in a rock group, he didn't approve of the music they were making. He didn't really believe that music was an essential part of who they were. He said that music should only be used to evangelize. As he spoke, Bono realized that this leader didn't understand what the group was trying to do. The band was trying to explore the relationship between

God and his people, not tell people what to believe and how to believe it.[42]

Bono, Edge, and Larry knew that they had come to a crossroads. Was the Shalom leader right? Did a commitment to God mean that they couldn't play rock music? Would certain works get them closer to heaven? Would a Mohawk or earrings keep them farther from it? For these three serious believers, the questions had to be answered so they could commit to a band. Or to God. Or to both.

But then the group came to a realization. "Where are these gifts coming from?" they wondered. "[Our music] is how we worship God, even though we don't write religious songs, because we [don't] feel God needs the advertising."[43]

Ultimately, all three men broke away from the Shalom group and its leader. "It was hard to leave," Bono admitted, but he knew he couldn't make the kind of music God had created him to make and remain in the group.[44]

The bandmates didn't have trouble reconciling the Bible's teaching with the music they played and the way they lived. *Other* people did. But U2 wasn't trying to satisfy other people. The only one they really wanted to please was God.

Love Explained

To some people, it seems strange that a rock star could love God, believe in the Bible, and sing prayers to an audience of thousands. But because of the amazing love of

Christ, that's just who Bono is. In 2006 Bono sat down with a reporter and explained exactly what God's love meant to him.

"My understanding of the Scriptures," said Bono, "has been made simple by the person of Christ. Christ teaches that God is love ... Love [is] a child born in straw poverty, the most vulnerable situation of all, without honor. I don't let my religious world get too complicated. I just kind of go: Well, I think I know what God is. God is love, and ... I respond in allowing myself to be transformed by that love and acting in that love. That's my religion. Where things get complicated for me, is when I try to live this love. Now that's not so easy.

"There's nothing hippie about my picture of Christ," Bono continued. "The Gospels paint a picture of a very demanding, sometimes divisive love, but love it is. I accept the Old Testament as more of an action movie: blood, car chases, evacuations, a lot of special effects, seas dividing, mass murder, adultery. The children of God are running amok, wayward. Maybe that's why they're so relatable. But the way we would see it, those of us who are trying to figure out our Christian conundrum, is that the God of the Old Testament is like the journey from stern father to friend. When you're a child, you need clear directions and some strict rules. But with Christ, we have access in a one-to-one relationship, for, as in the Old Testament, it was more one of worship and awe, a vertical relationship. The New Testament, on the other hand, we look across at a Jesus who looks familiar, horizontal. The combination is what makes the Cross.

Bono at London's Lyceum.

© Philip Grey/Lebrecht Music & Arts/Corbis

"It's a mind-blowing concept," he continued, "that the God who created the universe might be looking for company, a real relationship with people, but the thing that keeps me on my knees is the difference between grace and karma. You see, at the center of all religions is the idea of karma. You know, what you put out comes back to you: an eye for an eye, a tooth for a tooth, or in … physical laws, every action is met by an equal or an opposite one. It's clear to me that karma is at the very heart of the universe. I'm absolutely sure of it. And yet, along comes this idea called grace to upend all that 'as you reap, so you will sow' stuff. Grace defies reason and logic. Love interrupts ... the consequences of your actions, which in my case is very good news indeed, because I've done a lot of stupid stuff ... But I'd be in big trouble if karma was going to finally be my judge. It doesn't excuse my mistakes, but I'm holding out for grace. I'm holding out that Jesus took my sins onto the cross.

"The point of the death of Christ is that Christ took on the sins of the world, so that what we put out did not come back to us, and that our sinful nature does not reap the obvious death. That's the point. It should keep us humbled. It's not our own good works that get us through the gates of heaven."[45]

Living by grace and resting in the knowledge that Christ's death on the cross had already saved him, Bono was ready to take on the world.

Chapter 5

Limo Ride to the Circus

Embracing the States

The 1980s found U2 speeding on a road to wide new horizons, playing to larger audiences and pushing their musical boundaries. In March 1980, Island Records, a major record label, joined the band's adoring audience and signed them to a deal.

When the band's first album, *Boy*, was released, U2 hit the road. They booked fifty-six shows in the United Kingdom and traveled to continental Europe to perform for the first time. In December they went even further, taking their live show to the United States.

U2 had good reason to believe their soulful rock would appeal to America. America certainly appealed to Bono. For him, it was more than a country. It was a philosophy. "Everybody who values freedom, [forward] thinking, [and] innovation has a stake in America," Bono said. "The country [Americans] may own. But not the idea."[46]

Bono was ready to embrace the United States. The band flew into New York for a two-week tour.

The glittering city, the bustling traffic, the loud street talk all added to the buzz. (The excitement of this visit would inspire the song "Angel of Harlem" that appeared on their album *Rattle and Hum* eight years later.) To add to the thrill of the big city, the band's manager, Paul McGuiness, arranged a surprise: a limousine ride to the hotel.

"So here we were with no money," said Bono, "and [Paul] got the record company to do a *limousine!* Now, we'd never been in a limousine, we'd never been in New York, we'd never been in America. It was mind-blowing. So we all climb into this ridiculous-looking car with Christmas lights around the windows, and we're sitting there, laughing and giggling."[47]

When they finally settled into their hotel, Larry unrolled his sleeping bag onto the bed and promptly fell asleep. Bono couldn't fall asleep, though. He decided to turn on the TV, and the first program he saw had a televangelist preaching. In the flickering light of the screen, Bono sat and stared at the preacher.[48] He saw the people on the screen speaking his language, quoting the Bible. And yet something about it was all wrong. The televangelist sounded like a robot programmed to speak words without knowing their meaning.

Virginia Turbett/Redferns/Getty Images

U2 performing live onstage during the Boy Tour in 1980.

Bono was a believer. He understood the power of the Scriptures the televangelist was quoting. He believed in the healing power of faith. And the words the preacher was speaking sounded very similar to words that Bono himself used about God and the Bible. But Bono felt that he was seeing those words belittled and misinterpreted. As he watched, he remembered the story about Jesus turning over the tables of the moneylenders in Jerusalem's temple. Bono thought that the preacher on television was just like those moneylenders. He and the other televangelists were trampling on the most precious thing of all: God's love. Instead of bringing their viewers and listeners closer to faith, they were turning people away from God.[49]

This experience angered Bono. He was worried that if he used Christian language in America, people would think he was just another televangelist. It was a challenge Bono would meet.

Up the Charts

U2 returned to America when their album *Boy* was released in the United States. Their first good reviews meant the trip could be considerably longer than that first two-week stay.

Whenever he had a free moment in between all the concerts and interviews that filled up that sixty-performance tour, Bono wrote lyrics and composed melodies to get ready for the next album, which would eventually be titled *October*. They had already booked a studio to record the album, and the schedule was packed. But during a U2 performance in Portland, Oregon, Bono's case of musical notes was stolen.

The loss was devastating. Not only did the band have to start over with entirely new material, but the bill for the studio still had to be paid. They would have to start recording as scheduled, even though they had to write new music.

"I remember the pressure [the album] was made under," Bono would say later. Sometimes he would write lyrics to songs while he was standing at the microphone. He had to work quickly because the band was paying fifty pounds (about seventy-five dollars) per hour for the studio, and they couldn't waste any time. Nevertheless, the album came together. "The ironic thing about *October* is that there's a sort of peace about the album, even though it was recorded under that pressure," Bono said.

After that, every time Bono returned to Portland for a concert he would ask the audience for any information about that stolen briefcase and the music notes that were inside it. Finally, twenty-three years after losing the notes, a woman found the briefcase in the attic of a house she was renting. She returned the notes to Bono, who called this incident "an act of grace."[50]

In *October,* their second album, U2 covered new territory. The tracks highlighted piano, pipes, Larry's drums, and Adam's bass. Fans of *Boy* were surprised at *October,* and reviews were mixed. But Bono appreciated the band's fearlessness for choosing a different direction.

"A lot of people found *October* hard to accept at first," Bono said. "I think [the album] goes into areas that most rock 'n' roll bands ignore."

Even Bono, listening to it later, felt personally moved by one song in particular. Without even realizing what he was writing about, he composed a song called "Tomorrow." Listening to the song later, he realized that the song is really about his mother's funeral.

Much of Bono's inspiration, writing, and melodies have a sense of grace. The band sketched out ideas through hours of sweat and often fierce argument. But sometimes the harmony of the teamwork came together

Larry Mullen Jr., Bono, Adam Clayton, and The Edge, of the Irish rock band U2 pose in Dublin, April 17, 1980.

Paul Slattery/Retna UK /Landov

in something that Bono, Edge, Larry, and Adam could only call an inspired mystery.

But no one pretended that songwriting was easy. "If you know what *great* is, you know you're not it," Bono pointed out. "So you have to set up the opportunity to bump into it.... That's why songwriting by accident is so important, and ... getting to the place where that can happen, or as we say, getting to the place where God can walk through the room."[51]

U2 marched on with their third album, *War.* As they continued to explore new ground with political songs, it became their first #1 album in the United Kingdom. Audiences responded to the songs and the stage shows where Bono waved white flags. "Though our [record] is called *War*," Bono said, "the theme is very much surrender."[52]

As the front man of the band, Bono intentionally looked for a moment or a defining picture for people to respond to and grasp at a show. "It's like when you're writing," he explained, "you're looking all the time for the right image. Or when you're performing, you're looking for those moments." As a performer, Bono was never content with the distance between the crowd and the performer. He was always trying to cross that distance with the audience—both mentally and physically.[53]

By their fourth groundbreaking album, *The Unforgettable Fire*, U2's audiences had outgrown small clubs. *Rolling Stone* magazine named U2 the Band of the '80s, writing, "for a growing number of rock-and-roll fans, U2 has become the band that matters most, maybe even the only band that matters."

Around the Corner

In July 1985 U2 played Live Aid, a unique concert event for a greater cause. Presenting concerts all over the world, from London and Philadelphia, the "global jukebox" raised money for famine relief in Ethiopia. One hundred seventy thousand people saw the shows live. Four hundred million viewers across sixty countries caught it on TV. For bands, it was a major opportunity to showcase their music as well as encourage people to reach out in charity.

U2 played Live Aid at London's Wembley Stadium to an audience of 72,000 people. The band had prepared a set of three of their biggest hits. After "Sunday Bloody Sunday" got the huge crowd shouting and dancing, Bono said in the microphone, "We're an Irish band. We come from Dublin, a city in Ireland. Like all cities, it has its good; it has its bad. This is a song called 'Bad.'"

Looking out at the crowd as he sang, Bono found a meaningful moment. While the band played, he gestured to a young woman who was being pushed up against the front railing. When the ushers didn't respond, Bono leapt over a barrier, jumped ten feet down to the crowd, and motioned to the guards to pull her over the fence. As the band played on, Bono embraced the young woman and began to dance with her. The band *kept* playing, and the song stretched to fourteen minutes.

The strict time for their set ran out without the band performing their last song. As Bono's exit from the stage drained the time away, the other band members could only watch. Larry almost stopped playing altogether. For years after, he would joke that he thought Bono had gone out for tea and left them there.

Thinking the show had been a failure, Bono was devastated, certain that he had been responsible for what had gone wrong. "I wanted to find that moment," he said. "I got a terrible time from the band.... This was a big show for [us]. There were a billion people watching, and we didn't do our big song. Everyone was very annoyed with me, I mean, *very* annoyed."[54]

As it turned out, however, the event that seemed like a mistake played out on the news as the "breakthrough moment" for U2. The image of Bono dancing with a fan became the key picture for the entire Live Aid event. Audiences had witnessed the emotional and physical connection that the entertainer could make with an audience.

Their reputation as superstars on the live stage was cemented.

Chapter 6

Memories Tattooed on the Heart

Searching for Mercy

Moved by the experience of playing the Live Aid concert, Bono felt inspired to go to Africa and see the realities of life there in person. He couldn't get the thought of those suffering in Ethiopia out of his head. So he talked to his wife. "We have to try and do something," he told her. "In a quiet way." Ali agreed, and the couple decided to go to Africa. They didn't tell anyone they were going. There were no cameras or reporters following them around as they worked. They just went.[55]

In September, just two months after Bono played on a bright, worldwide stage, he and Ali slept in a tent for more than a month as they lived in Wello, Ethiopia. Working at a feeding station surrounded by barbed wire, they were in charge of the station's orphanage.

"In the morning," Bono recalled, "as the mist would lift, we would see thousands of people walking in lines toward the camp, people who had been walking for great distances through the night—men, women, children, families who'd lost everything, taking their few remaining possessions on a voyage to meet mercy."[56]

The heartbreak and despair of extreme poverty settled like the mist on their camp. One day a man walked up to Bono and held out a small child in his arms. "You take my son," the man said. "He'll live if you take him." Bono was dumbfounded. That moment, talking with the father of that child, formed Bono's commitment to Africa.

As Bono and Ali were flying home from Ethiopia on the plane, they agreed that neither of them would ever forget everything they had experienced in Africa.[57] The faces of children they had known and loved in Ethiopia were embedded in their hearts as deeply as tattoos. "Many things I swore I'd never forget that happened in that month," Bono said later. "You say you'll never forget but you get back to your daily life, you get back to the chores, you get back to your passions, but something stayed with me."[58]

Bono had fallen in love with the people of Africa. Love was making a move.

The following year Bono and Ali visited war-torn Central America. During their trip, they met mothers who had lost their children and villagers who had fled their ruined homes. Instead of going to work on this trip, they went to see for themselves the desperation that relief programs are up against. It didn't take long to see just how desperate the situation was.

One day during the visit, Bono and Ali went to an area controlled by a gang of rebels. They were crossing a road when they saw some soldiers on the other side. Bono noticed that the soldiers looked a little worried.

All of a sudden, there was a popping sound that whipped through the air over Bono's head. Everyone in the group froze. They could hear each other's hearts beating. Was it gunfire? Were they safe?

And then the soldiers started laughing. It wasn't a kind laugh. Bono said they were "letting us know that they don't like us and they could take our life if they really wanted to." Everyone was terrified, except the group leader. He didn't show any fear. "They're just trying to scare us," he said. "Keep walking. Not a problem."

Not a problem? thought Bono. *What's a problem? Grenades?*[59]

Just as Bono's trip to Ethiopia helped him understand extreme poverty and human suffering in a new way, his visit to Central America shed light on the complex nature of life in other countries. "Some images just overpower the eye," he said. "They just storm your brain and take prisoner of it. I have so many of those experiences. Sometimes I just don't want to share them ... It overpowers you in moments when you are really not expecting to. You find yourself walking down a street with tears rolling down your face. [There are] pictures that you can never be separate from."[60]

Songs from the Sadness

When Bono returned to the studio with U2, he did what came naturally to a writer with a melody: express his haunting memories in music. Two songs born out of his experiences, "Bullet the Blue Sky" and "Mothers of the Disappeared," were composed for U2's fifth studio album, *The Joshua Tree.*

In the middle of recording, more tragedy struck. Bono's assistant and friend Greg Carroll had died in a

Bono performs songs from *The Joshua Tree* album with folk singer Bob Dylan during a 1987 Inglewood, California, concert at the Forum.

motorcycle collision with a drunk driver. Bono had just arrived in America when he heard the news. "I had been in my hotel one hour after a thirteen-hour flight," he said. "I caught the next plane back to Dublin."[61]

Heartsick, Bono and Larry attended the traditional Maori funeral for Greg in his home country of New Zealand. They dedicated the new album to their lost mate and wrote the song "One Tree Hill" for him, named after a volcano in New Zealand.

With Bono's trips to poverty-stricken Ethiopia and war-torn Central America, it had been an especially difficult year for Bono. He described the year for himself and for the band as a "desert," and so U2 decided to use desert imagery for their new album.

The band went on a trip to the deserts of the southwestern United States to take pictures for the album. While there, they found an unusual tree growing all by itself, surrounded by oceans of sand. It was a Joshua tree. It is very unusual to find a Joshua tree by itself: this is a plant that usually grows in large groups. U2 was taken by the sight of this tree. The band filled the album's cover liner with black and white pictures of the tree and of sandy landscapes.

The Joshua Tree rose to the tops of the charts in twenty-two countries. It earned great critical reviews, sent four songs to the number-one spot, earned Grammy Awards for Album of the Year and Best Rock Performance, and landed U2 on the cover of *TIME* magazine as "Rock's Hottest Ticket." Selling 25 million copies, *The Joshua Tree* is still one of the world's all-time bestselling albums.

Bono sings on a Los Angeles rooftop during the filming of the video "Where the Streets Have No Name."

It was so popular that twenty years later, in 2007, U2 re-released the album for an anniversary edition. The success of the album shot the band members like human cannonballs on a wild circus ride.

U2 could play on any stage they wanted, anywhere in the world. But the stage they chose for their next act was a rooftop in Los Angeles, California.

Bono and the rest of the band set up their instruments and a huge sound system on the rooftop of a store. As a crowd gathered, they played eight songs to the delighted onlookers. The police, however, were not so delighted.

They said that U2 was creating a disturbance and demanded that they stop playing. They even shut off the power! But the band had come prepared with a backup generator, and Bono kept right on singing to the screaming, cheering crowd.

It wasn't easy for the band to follow the success of *The Joshua Tree*. Their next album was going to take lots of hard work and new ideas—something U2 had plenty of. Bono appreciated all the hard work—and the difficulties—that came along with working with Edge, Larry, and Adam. "Different points of view make you better," he said. "And the thing that'll make you less and less able to realize your potential is a room that's empty of argument."[62] All these different points of view and arguments eventually paid off: *Rattle and Hum* became one of the biggest albums of 1988.

In a way, this album paid tribute to the country that Bono had come to love: America. The band began to explore American music in all its diversity. The album has elements of blues, folk, and country, in addition to the rock 'n' roll sound that U2 had already established.

The band's last tour of the decade, the Lovetown Tour, ended in Dublin, back where it all began. At midnight on December 31, 1989, U2 opened their final show. They played "Where the Streets Have No Name" as the audience counted down the last seconds of the decade. Fans throughout Europe listened to the concert live on the radio.

After such a radical ride, where could Bono, Edge, Larry, and Adam possibly go? They were already at the

Bono sings the song "Elevation" during their Elevation Tour 2001 at the Molson Center in Montreal, Quebec, on October 12, 2001.

AP Images

very top of their profession. They were playing on the biggest stages in the world to the biggest crowds anyone could imagine. But Bono and the band thought there was still more work to be done.

The Joshua Tree had been U2's most successful album. Many critics and listeners felt that the band should continue writing, recording, and performing this same kind of music and never explore or experiment with different sounds and ideas. But that wasn't good enough for the band. They wanted to keep pushing and keep discovering what more they could do.

From the Dublin stage on that New Year's Eve, Bono told the audience what the band was going to do. "We've had a lot of fun over the last few months," he said into the mic, "just getting to know some of the music which we didn't know so much about—and still don't know very much about, but it was fun!... This is just the end of something for U2.... We have to go away and ... dream it all up again."

Chapter 7

Fresh Inspiration and a Side of Revenge

New Vibe

On Bono's 29th birthday, he received the best gift he could have imagined—his first daughter, Jordan. Bono was overwhelmed by the new mix of emotions he felt. Pride, love, and fear all surged through him at once. The greatest rock star in the world had been brought to his knees by a tiny baby. "I just felt this love for this beautiful little girl who was so fragile and so vulnerable," he said. "And I was very humbled to realize that."[63]

Bono's dad was as delighted as they were. Bono explained, "He loved kids, loved his grandchildren. His big thing, of course, was when I would have children, I would find out what it was like to be a father. The pain, the torture, et cetera. So when I went and told him that

Ali was pregnant, he burst out laughing. He couldn't stop laughing. I said: 'What are you laughing at?' He said: 'Revenge.' "[64]

In 1991 Bono and Ali welcomed their second daughter, Memphis Eve.

As Bono's family grew, the band discussed ending their partnership. After ten years of nonstop recording and performing, they needed to take a break from all the concerts and composing. Now, with families and other responsibilities dividing their attention, could they really maintain the intensity of creating another album? More importantly, did they believe they could be not just a great band, but the greatest band?

They did.

Making the next record, which they would eventually title *Achtung Baby*, proved harder than they thought. Because U2 had never followed "recipes for success," playing whatever kind of music was popular or had worked for them in the past, every record was like starting from scratch. They took kernels of ideas and grew them up through lots of hard work and deliberation. They played off each other's ideas and talents. Each member of the band made important contributions to the songs that were being written. And four musically talented, fiercely diverse individuals collaborating on an intense creative work always made for an intense process, even if it was rewarding in the end.

But the band was always pushing to do more, to be better. As they worked through a palette of ideas for the next album, they argued about design and sound.

Hoping to gain inspiration, they even started recording in Berlin. Just a few years earlier the city had been divided into two separate halves by a large wall guarded by soldiers. The east side of the city was controlled by the Soviet government, who kept strict control of their citizens and didn't allow them opportunities to live life as they wished. In 1989, the wall was torn down and Berlin became, once again, a unified city.

Bono, Edge, Larry, and Adam thought that recording in such a place would give them the inspiration they needed to start their next album. But instead of stimulating, bright ideas, they faced stifling darkness.

And then, as Bono said, "God walked through the room."

Improvising at the microphone, the four band members played a song that the whole world would come to know as "One."

"One" proved to be the creative breakthrough the band needed. Indeed, it has since been called one of the greatest songs of all time. U2 stayed up all night as they completed the recording in Dublin and finished their seventh studio album, *Achtung Baby* (which means "Attention Baby" in German). Little did they know that this album, which had been such a labor to create, would, in 2010, be voted the most influential record of the past twenty-five years.

Bono discussed the record in an interview. He said, "It's a con, in a way. We call it *Achtung Baby*, grinning up our sleeves in all the photography. But it's probably the heaviest record we've ever made."

Same U2, different packaging. *Achtung Baby* replaced *The Joshua Tree*'s obvious sincerity with self-mocking flash. In earlier years they had been criticized for being too serious and self-righteous. Bono and the rest of the band knew that their message was important, but they had to find a new way to say it.

The songs in *Achtung Baby* were certainly new for the band, but their concert tour, called Zoo TV, was an even bigger change. There were huge screens and big effects. The cool technology blended with mass media like it was on a caffeine overload. Video screens blitzed the senses with rapid special effects and pop-culture images. Through all this, the band was trying to show how technology and the media affect everyone's lives. The band criticized the greed and selfishness that had become so much a part of the world's culture. It was a radical departure for U2.

While Zoo TV's wild style never faded throughout the two-year tour, the show's details did change. Special guests made appearances. Most memorable, however, were the costumes in which Bono would appear.

These costumes were all about changing the delivery of the group's message. Just as the music and the stage design set a tone for the concert, the characters that Bono played twisted the audience's normal perceptions. When playing these characters, he would say things the audience knew he didn't mean, just to get his listeners to wake up and pay attention.

Sometimes Bono would dress up as The Fly. He wore leather pants and a leather coat, as well as big, dark sunglasses. This character was a typical rock star, strutting around the stage with a swagger and flair. The Fly could say things that Bono himself never would, which, in the end, gave Bono a greater freedom of speech.

On other occasions, Bono would appear as the Mirror Ball Man. In this costume, he wore a silver suit with matching boots and a cowboy hat. The Mirror Ball Man was a parody of greedy American televangelists (like the one who had angered Bono in that hotel room so long ago). When playing this character, Bono would speak in an exaggerated Southern accent. The Mirror Ball Man, said Bono, was the sort of man who would pick up a mirror, look at the reflection, and give the glass a big kiss. Most of all, this character loved money, thinking that financial success was a sign of God's blessing.

Finally, Bono would enter the stage dressed as Mr. MacPhisto. This character was a devil, complete with horns, a gold suit, and gold platform shoes. When dressed as Mr. MacPhisto, Bono would speak in an upper-class British accent. Edge said that Mr. MacPhisto "was a great device for saying the opposite of what you meant. It made the point so easily and with real humor." During concerts, Bono would make prank phone calls and take on the character of Mr. MacPhisto. Sometimes he would call local politicians who had made corrupt decisions. "When you're dressed as the Devil," said Bono, "your conversation is immediately loaded. If you tell somebody you really like what they're doing, you know it's not a compliment."

But these characters weren't all that was different about the Zoo TV tour. U2 even performed completely

Bono contemplates the destruction in the Sarajevo library on December 31, 1995, during a private visit to Sarajevo. Bono, who helped organize concerts in support of Sarajevo during the war, took advantage of peace to visit the city.

new songs, when, during a break in the tour, they released another album, called *Zooropa*.

And in some shows they interrupted the mocking tone of the concert to broadcast live, unscripted reality: satellite transmissions from war-torn Sarajevo, a city in Bosnia where different ethnic and religious groups had been at war for decades.

By the end of the ever-changing show, Bono had recorded and released U2's Grammy-winning album *Zooropa*, recorded a duet with legend Frank Sinatra, made prank calls to the White House, and fallen in love with a broken city in Bosnia.

Bono never forgot about this city, or how its endless conflict tugged at his heart. Several years later, he partnered with an American journalist who had participated in the Zoo TV Sarajevo satellite broadcasts. Together they created the award-winning documentary *Miss Sarajevo.*

The film focused on life in Sarajevo, the capital city of Bosnia, during a modern war. For four years, citizens in the city struggled to maintain an appearance of normality while gunfire from snipers exploded across the rooftops, and while they went for months without running water or electricity.

In the disquieting theme song of the documentary, Bono merged opera and rock into a haunting melody. In 1995 U2 performed it with opera legend Luciano Pavarotti in Modena, Italy. Another live performance wouldn't happen again until they sang it for the war-torn city itself.

Popped

U2's next album, *Pop,* explored new technology and surveyed new sounds. Creative discovery and development takes time, however, and the album got hung up in the recording studio. While some deadlines can be delayed, the 1997 tour schedule was not one of them. Tickets to upcoming concerts had already been sold. The show had to go on.

Bono and Luciano Pavarotti perform at the Pavarotti and Friends concert on May 27, 2003, in Modena, Italy.

Opening in Las Vegas, Nevada, the PopMart Tour poked fun at popular culture and the consumerist concept of *Buy! More! Now!* Bono didn't wave white flags on this tour as he had during the concerts for *War.* In quite a different picture—which was sometimes misunderstood and sometimes dismissed—the show's message was ironic, extravagant, and deliberately over-the-top.

Ultimately the band's recording time intruded on rehearsals for the live shows, affecting studio *and* live sessions. The music wasn't really where they wanted it to be, and the ambitious, oversized shows suffered a host of technical difficulties. One of these difficulties always seemed to involve a giant revolving mirror-ball lemon.

At the end of the concerts, the band would begin their encores by emerging from this lemon. The lemon didn't always work the way it should, however, and twice the band got stuck in the fruit. Bono was able to laugh about it later. "I still miss our lemon," he said. "That was a beautiful, psychedelic kind of funky. It was a beautiful thing, traveling in that lemon."

The band had spent most of the 1990s deconstructing their serious image but not entirely abandoning it. The music they made could still electrify their listeners and liberate their hearts. In the middle of the PopMart Tour, U2 brought the music to war-torn Sarajevo. They were the first band able to host a concert there after war ravaged the city, and they tried to include all ethnic groups in the 50,000-person crowd. Trains were running for the first time in years, just to bring people to see the concert.

U2's Sarajevo performance was big and bold—live rock stars with soft hearts. Fittingly, they included a special rendition of "Miss Sarajevo" in their set.

Bono later called the Sarajevo show "one of the toughest and one of the sweetest nights of my life." For the city, it was pure love. "For two magical hours," one news story reported, "the rock band U2 achieved what warriors, politicians, and diplomats could not: They united Bosnia."

The Sarajevo show remained an emotional highlight in an otherwise difficult tour. The tour brought in a lot of money, but it cost even more to produce. U2 actually risked going bankrupt to do the tour.

Stripping It All Away

While U2 was in danger of bankruptcy, Bono focused on a different kind of deal. "I think celebrity is ridiculous, but it's currency. We try to spend ours wisely. We try to put it to some use."[65]

This was certainly true when Bono became a spokesman for the Jubilee 2000 campaign. This campaign put him shoulder to shoulder with power brokers, like former US President Bill Clinton and British Prime Minister Tony Blair. Bono argued that the new millennium was the ideal time to release the world's poorest countries from their debts so they could pay for health care for their people.

Whenever a country borrows money, it is required to pay back the original amount *plus interest*. For every dollar countries in Africa were borrowing, they owed back eight dollars—a backbreaking amount even for a wealthy nation, let alone a poor one. Most of the money African nations were receiving from foreign aid, then, was going to paying previous loans instead of supporting the starving, hurting people who needed the money most. Bono knew that this was wrong, and he wanted to do something about it.

Under the demands of a taxing schedule, Bono spent much of his time working for the success of Jubilee 2000 and then flying back to Dublin to join the band in the studio.

With each new album, U2 sought to create fresh music that was original, unique, and relevant. And, as had come to be expected, recording sessions took longer than they had planned (in no small part because of Bono's busy schedule). But this time, unlike with *Pop*, U2 refused to be rushed, and they postponed the release of the record. The group stepped back from the extravagance of their earlier experimentation and returned to writing songs with strong melodies. Taking away all the glitter from alternative techno sounds, U2 stripped the music down to its essence.

Anxious fans had to wait months before they could hear the band's new music, but when the finished product was released in October 2000, listeners weren't disappointed. *All That You Can't Leave Behind* debuted at number one in twenty-two countries.

The album's simple black-and-white cover art reflected the straightforward, sometimes understated sound as well. The photograph on the cover of the album shows the band standing in an airport, as if waiting to depart. A sign directing passengers to the correct gate originally read *F21–36,* but Bono had the photo changed so the sign read *J33–3.* This was in reference to the Bible verse Jeremiah 33:3: "Call to me and I will answer you and tell you great and unsearchable things you do not know." Bono referred to it as God's own phone call. (Jeremiah 33:3 would make another appearance in the lyric "3:33 when the numbers fell off the clock face" on the intimate worship song "Unknown Caller" from the group's 2009 album *No Line on the Horizon.*)

Bono and Ali's third child, Elijah Bob Patricius Guggi Q, had been born on their seventeenth wedding anniversary, before the album was released. Like a bookend, their fourth child, John Abraham, was born after the release, just as the Elevation Tour was getting under way.

Five months later, Bono's dad was admitted to the hospital in the last stages of cancer. Bono went to be with him.

"I got to make peace with him, but never really to become his friend," Bono said. The two men were never really able to talk together. In his last days, Bono would visit him every day in the hospital, but all his father could do was whisper.

Bono spent many evenings lying beside his father on a roll-up bed. Since the older man couldn't speak, few words passed between father and son. While Bono sat there with his father, he drew pictures. Sometimes he drew pictures of his father's hospital room, complete with all the wires and tubes. And sometimes he would read to his father. Bob loved the rich language of Shakespeare, and Bono read plays to the dying man.[66]

After his father died, Bono went onstage in London to continue the European tour and to pay tribute to his dad. "We all want to thank my old man for giving me this voice," Bono said at one of these concerts. "He was a fine tenor, and said to me if only I'd had [his] voice, just think what could [have happened]." Then he sang "Kite," a song Bono had written for his own children. "This is for you, Bob," he said.[67]

The tribute spoke volumes about Bono's love for his father. Even if things were never perfect between them,

Bono would always cherish the memory of his dad. "I suppose I didn't have a great relationship with my father for a long time," Bono said. "I . . . made peace with him before he died, but I wished I had put that right earlier."[68]

All those emotions showed up in the music. Bono's personal tribute to his dad came on the next U2 album, *How To Dismantle An Atomic Bomb.*

"His demise set me off on a journey, a rampage, a desperate hunt to find out who I was," Bono explained, "and that resulted in a lot of these songs."

Specifically, "Sometimes You Can't Make It On Your Own" was inspired by Bono's dad, the macho Irish opera lover. The heartfelt tribute went on to win Song of the Year at the 2006 Grammy Awards.

"This is for you, Bob."

Chapter 8

What This Team Needs Is a Rock Star

The Crisis and the Emergency

As a musician who has stayed in the same band for decades while also partnering with artists from opera, R&B, rap, folk, country, and rock, Bono understands the power of working together.

It is little wonder that he searches out meaningful partnerships that will help bring mercy to the world in practical, measurable ways.

Bono has, in a sense, stopped trying to use his music for political purposes. He still performs in sold-out stadiums, but he knows he can do more good for Africa by working closely with world leaders and talking about the problems the continent faces. "I'm tired of dreaming," he says. "I'm into doing at the moment. It's like, let's only have goals that we can go after. U2 is about the impossible. Politics is the art of the possible. They're very different, and I'm resigned to that now."

"Two-and-a-half million Africans are going to die next year for the stupidest of reasons: because it's difficult to get the AIDS drugs to them," Bono said. "Well, it's not difficult to get fizzy drinks to the furthest ... reaches of Africa. We can get cold, fizzy drinks. Surely we can get the drugs. This is America. We can do anything here. You've got a guy on the moon. You know what I mean?"[69]

Receiving the right medication affects not just whether a child lives or how well he lives, but also how well he learns. Health and education are linked. Treat the illness—AIDS or malaria or lice—and schools and learning are no longer a distant dream. "In the not-too-distant future," says Bono, "the rich world will invest in the education of the poor world, because it is our best protection against young minds being twisted by extremist ideologies—or growing up without any ideology at all, which could be worse.

"I'm arguing for a demonstration to the world of what we're capable of in the West, with our technology, our innovations, our agriculture, our pharmacology," said Bono. "We've developed this unimaginable prosperity. Let's show the world what we can do with it."[70]

The AIDS emergency isn't the only thing that has Bono working overtime. Helping impoverished people includes forgiving national debts so countries can develop their own resources, build roads and schools, get

AP Images

President George W. Bush shakes hands with Bono, right, after Bush spoke at the Inter-American Development Bank, March 14, 2002, in Washington.

medicine to the sick, and raise up a generation free from the endless cycle of poverty.

Bono understands the force he commands as an individual. He walks onto a stage and the planet pays attention. He knows how to communicate a message. And he will not back down from a fight — especially when it's a fight he believes in.

With his unique and powerful voice, Bono has mobilized the effort to help the world's poorest. But he knows it's a mission that can't be done alone.

Good Deals

For Africa, Bono had to make new collaborations with talents that had nothing to do with music. After all, partnerships can't be forged only with one's friends. "You don't have to be harmonious on everything—just one thing—to get along with someone," Bono pointed out.[71]

Former US Treasury Secretary Paul O'Neill had a common response to the singer that knocked on his door. "I refused to meet him at first," O'Neill said. "I thought he was just some pop star who wanted to use me." But eventually he agreed to sit down and talk with Bono. They talked for an hour and a half, and the treasury secretary changed his opinion. "He's a serious person. He cares deeply about these issues, and you know what? He knows a lot about them."[72]

Bono also talked to then-President Bill Clinton and others, showing how canceling debt can reduce poverty while increasing goodwill toward America.

At a meeting of the world's most powerful heads of government in 2005 (in what would come to be called the G8 Summit), Bono helped convince industrial nations to forgive over $40 billion in African loans. "These countries, instead of paying ... old debts can spend it on ... health, education, and infrastructure," he

Former President Bill Clinton speaks with Bono before a dinner in New York in honor of the Frank Foundation Child Assistance International of Washington, D.C.

argued. And the heads of state listened. They promised to give access to medicine to almost ten million impoverished people with HIV.[73]

But Bono didn't stop there. He proceeded to seek out then-President George W. Bush and National Security Adviser Condoleeza Rice. "People openly laughed in my face when I suggested that this administration would distribute antiretroviral drugs to Africans," Bono said. "They said, 'You are out of your tiny mind.'" But Bono remained persistent, and eventually the administration listened. They promised an astonishing gift of $500 million to help stop the spread of AIDS in Africa. "There [are] 200,000 Africans now who owe their lives to America," Bono said proudly.[74]

In his mission, Bono also toured four African countries with US Treasury Secretary O'Neill. He appealed to Canadian prime ministers, statesmen, and four-star generals.

"If you put your shoulder to the door, it might open," said Bono, "especially if you're representing a greater authority than yourself. Call it love, call it justice, call it whatever you want ... Most will agree that if there is a God, God has a special place for the poor. The poor are where God lives. So these politicians should be nervous, not me."[75]

Bono worked with politicians and world leaders on all sides of different political issues. But once again, Bono wasn't willing to stop there. So he went into the church. He reached into the pews and urged those who listened not to stay quiet and meek in the face of such extreme famine and poverty. "God will not accept that," Bono said at an annual prayer breakfast. "Mine won't, at least. Will yours?"[76]

Motivated by a higher calling, the church took steps to mobilize its massive organization with medicine and mosquito nets that prevent malaria. But not every Christian group got behind the efforts. Many conservative congregations responded weakly, ignoring the struggles of distant Africans with whom they felt they shared little common ground. Bono was furious.

"I was very angry that conservative Christians were not involved more in the AIDS emergency," Bono said. "I was saying, 'This is the leprosy that we read in the New Testament. Christ hung out with the lepers but you're ignoring the AIDS emergency. How can you?'" This time, the conservative Christians listened. They agreed that they needed to be involved in the AIDS crisis, and they began to fund missions to Africa.[77]

Bono also talked with Oprah Winfrey—and her millions of viewers—explaining what was happening in Africa, and how easy it would be for Americans to help change the world. "For the same price of taking your girlfriend to the movies," he said, "you can change their lives. What a privilege to be in that situation."[78]

All this work brought with it a sober realization that the more partners Bono had in this work, the better. "The problem just has to be sorted and we can't do it just with governments alone," he said. "We're fighting a fire. The house is burning down. Let's get the water. You end up beside somebody who lives up the road who you don't really like. Do you really care if he's polishing up his image [by] putting the fire out?"[79]

Bono has worked tirelessly to rally partners so that love can change the world. It's a huge mission, but in the end, Bono believes that a better world is possible. "It's always the same attitude that wins the day: faith over fear. On the Africa stuff we can't lose, because we're putting our shoulder to a door God Almighty has already opened."[80]

From the Stage

Since Bono leaped from the stage at the Live Aid concert in 1985, U2 has used its shows to motivate and mobilize audiences for humanitarian causes.

When the group highlighted human rights work during Amnesty International's Conspiracy of Hope, the organization's membership in the United States grew by 45,000 people.

When they protested a nuclear factory in the United Kingdom in a concert, all proceeds went to Greenpeace.

In 2003, U2 went onstage during the Special Olympics to perform "One" and "Pride (In The Name Of Love)." At the end, Nelson Mandela joined the group onstage as a symbol of unity.

Bono also helped organize a series of benefit concerts for the world's poorest countries. Describing these concerts, Bono explained that Live Aid in the 1980s had been about charity. These concerts were about justice. "There's a reason why these people are stuck," he said, "aside from corruption and natural calamity, both of which you find on the African continent — but there are other reasons we're involved in why these people can't get up off their knees." So in July 2005, U2 performed to spotlight the crises of nations facing the AIDS epidemic.

In 2009, U2 performed in Germany to celebrate the twentieth anniversary of the day when the wall

Juda Ngwenya/Reuters/Landov

Bono and former South African president Nelson Mandela pose after they met at Mandela's residence in Johannesburg, May 25, 2002.

that divided East and West Berlin came tumbling down. Their concert at the Brandenburg Gate celebrated the day in November, 1989, when freedom reclaimed the city. "Happy birthday, Berlin!" Bono called out at the concert.

Whether for Africa or Sarajevo, Bono's gifts have turned a voice into an appeal and a song into a calling. To communicate with a crowd or to partner with a politician you don't necessarily need a rock star—but if you want to move mountains, it doesn't hurt to have this one.

"What makes you qualified to help a person who has been knocked down in a car accident?" Bono asked. "There's only one qualification necessary: that you happened to be there, and you happened to be able to call the ambulance. That's really how I see my role: as raising the alarm."[81]

Chapter 9

Rock It Like You Mean It

Moving Target

In the thirty years U2 has been together, their music has stayed at the top of the charts. They've remained real and current by speaking to each generation, by riding the waves of change instead of swimming in one place.

Entertainment technology is changing fast, but U2 is keeping up. MP3 players, iPods, mobile phones, and other digital music devices have changed how people listen to their music. Having fans who listen to a whole, unified album, with each song building on the last to form a theme, is increasingly rare.

Coming up with great music is no longer enough. These days *what* Bono sings or says is just as important as *how* he chooses to say it. "We have to start thinking about new ways of getting our songs across," Bono said, "of communicating in this new world, with so many channels."[82]

In 2006, a group of filmmakers approached U2. They had an idea about making a concert film that involved state-of-the-art 3D technology. It was a huge project that threatened to distract them from their Vertigo Tour. But U2 ended up taking the chance to be part of a cutting-edge experiment.

After shooting seven concerts in Latin America and two in Australia, *U23D* was released in 2008. It was the first film shot, produced, and screened entirely in 3D. The eleventh-highest grossing concert film of all time, it holds a spot right below U2's 1988 film *Rattle and Hum*.

The band broke new ground on their 2010 concert film as well. Twenty-seven high definition cameras were used to film *U2 360 at the Rose Bowl* in Pasadena, California. The same concert holds the distinction as the first one ever to be streamed live on YouTube.

Their hit "Vertigo" got some unusual airtime—on a television commercial for iPods. The ad looked more like a music video than a commercial. But some critics accused the band of selling out. They said that the band had diminished their music by using it for commercials. These critics thought that when fans heard the song on the radio, they would associate it with an advertisement instead of what it was really trying to say.

Bono disagreed. *"Selling out* is doing something you don't really want to do for money," he argued. "That's what selling out is. We asked to be in the ad. We could

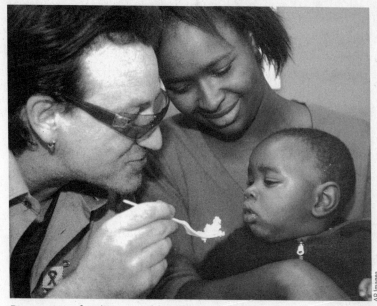

Bono spoon-feeds 11-month-old Thomas Qubile while his mother, Mpumelelo, looks on at the prenatal HIV clinic of the Chris Hani Baragwanath Hospital in Soweto, South Africa.

see where rock music is, fighting for relevance next to hip-hop."[83]

Agree with the move or not, a lot of young kids could now sing along with "Vertigo" even if they'd never heard of U2 and didn't know about the band's collection of Grammy Awards or their induction into the Rock and Roll Hall of Fame. For a new generation, "Vertigo" was the beginning of a lifelong relationship with U2. "If you pour your life into songs, you want them to be heard," said Bono. "It's a desire to communicate. A deep desire to communicate inspires songwriting."

At the same time, the band is not interested in writing jingles—or anything that resembles them. U2 was once offered twenty-three million dollars for the music rights to one of their biggest, most recognizable anthems: "Where the Streets Have No Name." A car company wanted to make a commercial using the song. "I know from my work in Africa what $23 million could buy," Bono said. "It was very hard to walk away from $23 million." But the band knew that if a show was ever a little bit off—if the crowd wasn't energized and their music wasn't sounding the way they wanted it to—they could play "Where the Streets Have No Name" and, as Bono said, God would walk through the room. That was the one song they could rely on to change the mood of an audience and bring their hearts back to the music. Bono, Edge, Larry, and Adam agreed that they didn't want people in the audience to turn to each other when they heard the opening riff of the song and say, "Oh, now they're playing the car commercial." The band turned down the offer.[84]

Thirty-year friends Bono, Edge, Larry, and Adam want to stay in the band as long as it means staying consistent without being stagnant, pushing creative limits but not losing themselves, and arguing but working toward the same goals. Speaking about his partnership with his three extraordinary friends and bandmates, Bono said, "I want to see what can happen with a band if they keep their integrity, keep their commitment to each other, and ... create extraordinary music ... [What if we] actually stayed in contact with the world, were awake, [and] didn't let the money buy [us] off, you know? I'm still hungry. I still want a lot out of the music."[85]

New Heights

After the 2004 album *How to Dismantle an Atomic Bomb*, Bono revealed that once again, U2 would go in a different musical direction. "We're going to continue to be a band, but maybe the rock will have to go; maybe the rock has to get a lot harder. But whatever it is, it's not gonna stay where it is."

Not only did they experiment musically, but Bono experimented writing songs from another point of view, like that of a police officer or a soldier. "It's a very personal album," Bono said. "These are very personal stories even though they are written in character and, in a way, they couldn't be further from my own politics. But, in the sense of the peripheral vision, there's a world out there."

In February 2009, U2 released their twelfth studio album, *No Line on the Horizon*. It took five years, three producers, more than fifty song concepts, and studios in four different countries.

The subsequent tour, called the 360 Tour, took the group's performance experimentation to new heights as well. The tour's centerpiece—a massive, specially designed stage nicknamed the Claw—was part spaceship and part giant claw. It allowed the band to set up in the middle of a stadium and be surrounded by the fans.

AP Images

Lead singer Bono, center, and the rock band U2 perform during their 360° Tour at Wembley Stadium in London, Friday, Aug. 14, 2009.

The tour's show in the Rose Bowl Stadium in Pasadena, California, set the record for the highest attendance for a United States show by one headliner. (The previous record holder was *also* U2, set in 1987.) By the end of the 360 Tour, they will have played to nearly six million people.[86]

In the midst of all the work to be done in his humanitarian efforts, Bono still loves the stage, playing with the guys and giving expression to the melodies in his head. "Over the years, you ... take for granted the opportunity to make music," he said. "I'm very happy as an activist, but it's a very demanding life, a slog, and it can be dirty work. This record put me back in the place I was as a teenager, working in a gas station, dreaming of getting to rehearsal with the band. It was so intoxicating to hear an electric guitar or the silver sound of a cymbal. Maybe I needed to be reminded of that."[87]

What Is Possible

The accomplishments of an Irish musician and his three band mates are testimony to what can happen when people seek to do the extraordinary. "Don't get too interested in what's possible,'" Bono said. "The impossible is made possible by a combination of faith, gift, and strategy."[88]

In their long and continuing career, U2 has won twenty-two Grammys, including Best Rock Group, Best Rock Album, Album of the Year, Record of the Year, and Song of the Year. In 2005 they were inducted into the Rock and Roll Hall of Fame. Their work has lingered on top-ten charts all over the world and has won a truckload of international awards. And they've sold enough albums to give a copy to each person in Ireland—and then do it again twenty-nine times.

Bono's list of personal honors runs as long as a U2 hit list. He has been nominated for the Nobel Peace Prize three different times, has been named a Knight of the Legion of Honour in France, granted honorary knighthood in the United Kingdom, and named *TIME* magazine's Person of the Year in 2005. In 2010 he was awarded

Bono claps palms with Maasai children during his visit to the traditional Shambasha village near Arusha, Tanzania, during a six-nation tour of Africa.

the Humanitarian Leadership Award for his work with The ONE Campaign, which continues to rally resources and awareness to fight disease and poverty in Africa. In many ways, this is Bono's life work. "On so many issues it's difficult to know what God wants from us," Bono said, "but on this issue, helping the desperately poor, we know God will bless it."[89]

And the blessings are being felt like ripples across an ocean. "As a result of debt cancellation, there are an extra forty million children going to school on the continent of Africa," Bono stated.[90] And seemingly impossible strides in health care have been made. "There was a time when no Africans could afford those little drugs—two pills a day is all it takes to keep you alive, and people are dying—five thousand a day. Now there are three million Africans on antiretroviral drugs."[91]

He is a man on a mission in a band on a mission. And the other band members are glad that he's still making music. "The good news from our point of view is that he prefers working on music more than anything else," says Edge. "And also he's unelectable."[92]

As a man who has sought to reconcile tragedy and love, stardom and compassion, this son of a Dublin postal worker has followed faith and music in a continuing thread. The music courses through Bono's veins and runs through his heart. So does the haunting memory of a man carrying his son in Ethiopia—*If you take him, he will live.*

Just as U2's music has become bigger than the four men who make it, Bono's work in Africa and other impoverished nations is bigger than any one man. "What I'm hoping," he says, "is that the social movement that is growing around our issues will be so strong that in the event of somebody like me not being around, they won't notice. In the end, social movements carry the day, not rock stars."[93]

Until then, there's Bono.

Endnotes

1. Tyrangiel, Josh. "Bono's Mission." Posted February 23, 2002. *TIME Magazine Online. www.time.com.*

2. Eckstrom, Kevin. "Bono, After Years of Skepticism, Finds Partner in Religion." Posted February 3, 2006. *Religion News Service. www.atu2.com.*

3. Tyrangiel, Josh. "Bono's Mission." Posted February 23, 2002. *TIME Magazine Online. www.time.com.*

4. Wenner, Jann S. "Bono: The Rolling Stone Interview." *Rolling Stone Magazine* 986 (November 3, 2005).

5. Bono. Interview by Larry King. *Larry King Weekend.* CNN, December 1, 2002.

6. Assayas, Michka. *Bono: In Conversation with Michka Assayas.* New York: Berkley Publishing Group (2006), 124.

7. Fry, Maddy. "Bono Biography." *www.atu2.com.*

8. Bono. Interview by Larry King. *Larry King Weekend.* CNN, December 1, 2002.

9. Assayas, Michka. *Bono: In Conversation with Michka Assayas.* New York: Berkley Publishing Group (2006), 14.

10. Wenner, Jann S. "Bono: The Rolling Stone Interview." *Rolling Stone Magazine* 986 (November 3, 2005).

11. Assayas, Michka. *Bono: In Conversation with Michka Assayas.* New York: Berkley Publishing Group (2006), 18.

12. Fry, Maddy. "Bono Biography." *www.atu2.com.*

13. Assayas, Michka. *Bono: In Conversation with Michka Assayas.* New York: Berkley Publishing Group (2006), 13.

14. Bono. Interview by Larry King. *Larry King Weekend.* CNN, December 1, 2002.

15. Wenner, Jann S. "Bono: The Rolling Stone Interview." *Rolling Stone Magazine* 986 (November 3, 2005).

16. Assayas, Michka. *Bono: In Conversation with Michka Assayas.* New York: Berkley Publishing Group (2006), 22–23.

17. Ibid., 271.

18. Wenner, Jann S. "Bono: The Rolling Stone Interview." *Rolling Stone Magazine* 986 (November 3, 2005).

19. Ibid.

20. Ibid.

21. Assayas, Michka. *Bono: In Conversation with Michka Assayas.* New York: Berkley Publishing Group (2006), 56.

22. Wenner, Jann S. "Bono: The Rolling Stone Interview." *Rolling Stone Magazine* 986 (November 3, 2005).

23. Ibid.

24. Ibid.

25. Assayas, Michka. *Bono: In Conversation with Michka Assayas.* New York: Berkley Publishing Group (2006), 55–56.

26. Ibid., 13.

27. Ibid., 57.

28. Ibid.

29. Ibid., 132.

30. Ibid.

31. DeCurtis, Anthony. "The Rolling Stone Interview: Bono." *Rolling Stone Magazine,* October 30, 2007.

32. Assayas, Michka. *Bono: In Conversation with Michka Assayas.* New York: Berkley Publishing Group (2006), 69–70.

33. Bono. Interview by Larry King. *Larry King Weekend.* CNN, December 1, 2002.

34. Ibid.

35. Assayas, Michka. *Bono: In Conversation with Michka Assayas*. New York: Berkley Publishing Group (2006), 131.

36. Interview with Bono, August 20, 1983. *www.youtube.com*.

37. Wenner, Jann S. "Bono: The Rolling Stone Interview." *Rolling Stone Magazine* 986 (November 3, 2005).

38. O'Connor, Brendan. "U2: Access All Areas." Posted June 21, 2009. *The Independent. www.independent.ie*.

39. Wenner, Jann S. "Bono: The Rolling Stone Interview." *Rolling Stone Magazine* 986 (November 3, 2005).

40. Assayas, Michka. *Bono: In Conversation with Michka Assayas*. New York: Berkley Publishing Group (2006), 162.

41. Ibid., 163.

42. Ibid., 162–163.

43. Ibid., 163.

44. Ibid.

45. Ibid., 226–227.

46. Bono. Interview by John Kasich. *Heartland with John Kasich*. Fox News, March 26, 2007.

47. Assayas, Michka. *Bono: In Conversation with Michka Assayas*. New York: Berkley Publishing Group (2006), 183.

48. Ibid., 186.

49. Ibid.

50. "U2 Lyrics Returned After 23 Years." Posted October 22, 2004. *BBC News. www.bbc.co.uk*.

51. Assayas, Michka. *Bono: In Conversation with Michka Assayas*. New York: Berkley Publishing Group (2006), 178.

52. "Interview with Bono, August 20, 1983." *www.youtube.com*.

53. Assayas, Michka. *Bono: In Conversation with Michka Assayas*. New York: Berkley Publishing Group (2006), 232.

54. Ibid., 233.

55. Ibid., 248.

56. Ibid., 247.

57. "Oprah Talks to Bono." Posted April 15, 2004. *O Magazine Online*. *www.oprah.com*.

58. Bono. Interview by John Kasich. *Heartland with John Kasich*. Fox News, March 26, 2007.

59. Assayas, Michka. *Bono: In Conversation with Michka Assayas*. New York: Berkley Publishing Group (2006), 201–202.

60. Ibid., 210–211.

61. Joseph, Carolus. "Irish Band U2 Come to Tangi (Funeral)." Posted February 5, 2009. *NZ Rock 'n' Roll History Online*. *www.kiwirock.co.nz*.

62. Assayas, Michka. *Bono: In Conversation with Michka Assayas*. New York: Berkley Publishing Group (2006), 169.

63. Ibid., 148.

64. Ibid., 25.

65. "U2 Uncovered." Interview by Cat Deely. ITV2, 2005. *www.youtube.com*.

66. Assayas, Michka. *Bono: In Conversation with Michka Assayas*. New York: Berkley Publishing Group (2006), 11.

67. "Bono Pays Tribute to Dad at U2 Concert." Posted August 22, 2001. *ABC News Online*. *www.abcnews.go.com*.

68. Bono. Interview by Larry King. *Larry King Weekend*. CNN, December 1, 2002.

69. Ibid.

70. "The Rolling Stone Interview: Bono." *Rolling Stone Magazine,* October 30, 2007.

71. Assayas, Michka. *Bono: In Conversation with Michka Assayas*. New York: Berkley Publishing Group (2006), 104.

72. Tyrangiel, Josh. "Bono's Mission." Posted February 23, 2002. *TIME Magazine Online*. *www.time.com*.

73. Bono. Interview by Ed Bradley. *60 Minutes*, CBS, 2005.

74. Assayas, Michka. *Bono: In Conversation with Michka Assayas*. New York: Berkley Publishing Group (2006), 138.

75. Ibid., 137–138.

76. Eckstrom, Kevin. "Bono, After Years of Skepticism, Finds Partner in Religion." Posted February 3, 2006. *Religion News Service. www.atu2.com.*

77. Bono. Interview by Ed Bradley. *60 Minutes*, CBS, 2005.

78. Bono. Interview by Oprah Winfrey. *The Oprah Winfrey Show.* CBS, September 20, 2002.

79. Dakss, Brian. "Bono Seeing 'Red' Over AIDS." Posted January 26, 2006. *The Early Show Online. www.cbsnews.com.*

80. Assayas, Michka. *Bono: In Conversation with Michka Assayas.* New York: Berkley Publishing Group (2006), 105.

81. Bono. Interview by Greg Kot. "Transcript of Bono Interview." *Chicago Tribune,* May 13, 2005.

82. Ibid.

83. Ibid.

84. Ibid.

85. Bono. Interview by Ed Bradley. *60 Minutes*, CBS, 2005.

86. "Bono, U2 Adapt to Changing Times." Posted October 23, 2009. *CBS News Online. www.cbsnews.com.*

87. Gundersen, Edna. "'Horizon' Evolves with U2's Audacity, Creativity, Innovation." Posted March 1, 2009. *USA Today Online. www.usatoday.com.*

88. DeCurtis, Anthony. "The Rolling Stone Interview: Bono." *Rolling Stone Magazine,* October 30, 2007.

89. Tyrangiel, Josh. "The Constant Charmer." Posted December 19, 2005. *TIME Magazine Online. www.time.com.*

90. Bono. "Who Let the Peacenik In?" (Speech given at the Atlantic Council, Washington, DC, April 29, 2010). *www.u2.com.*

91. Interview with Bono in Fez, Morocco (part 3). Posted on March 25, 2009. *www.youtube.com.*

92. Tyrangiel, Josh. "The Constant Charmer." Posted December 19, 2005. *TIME Magazine Online. www.time.com.*

93. DeCurtis, Anthony. "The Rolling Stone Interview: Bono." *Rolling Stone Magazine,* October 30, 2007.

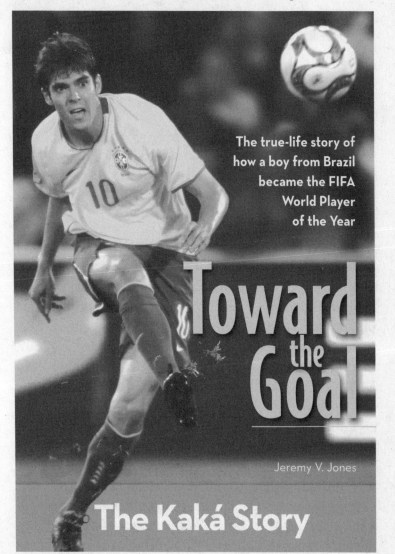

The true-life story of
how a boy from Brazil
became the FIFA
World Player
of the Year

Toward
the
Goal

Jeremy V. Jones

The Kaká Story

1

A Champion Among Champions

It was the biggest game of the year. The winner would be the champion of all of Europe's mighty professional leagues and teams. Soccer clubs across the continent had played each other all season long in the ongoing UEFA Champions League tournament. Now, on May 23, 2007, in approximately ninety minutes of soccer, Italy's A.C. Milan or England's Liverpool would be crowned the best of the best.

Police in riot gear ringed the outside of Olympic Stadium in Athens, Greece. At one point fans without tickets tried to break down a closed gate to storm their way, and the police fired tear gas to repel them.

But the true battle was taking place on the brilliant green grass rectangle at the center of the stadium. Seventy thousand cheering, chanting fans watched as the action unfolded in red and white before them. Milan wore white; Liverpool red.

Liverpool took control of the action early, and the Reds' Jermaine Pennant got the first shot on goal eight minutes in. But Milan's goalkeeper, Dida, made the diving save.

Once Milan settled down the game was evenly matched, and neither side could break through the other's tough defense. It seemed as if the two coaches had prepared their teams so well that the defenses could anticipate every attack.

The Milan team was filled with veteran World Cup winners and European Champions such as Paolo Maldini and Clarence Seedorf, but its superstar was young number twenty-two: Kaká. It was his heroic play in the semifinal game that had secured the victory over Manchester United and propelled the *Rossoneri* (Milan's nickname, referring to their red and black uniforms) to this final game.

Liverpool was well aware of the threat Kaká posed, and used its defensive midfielder Javier Mascherano to dog Milan's most creative playmaker and pressure him constantly. The tactic seemed to work. Kaká and his whole team mustered only one shot on goal during the first half, and it was easily saved by Liverpool's keeper Pepe Reina.

A minute before halftime, Kaká was fouled just outside of Liverpool's penalty area, giving a free kick to Milan. Their free kick specialist Andrea Pirlo placed the silver and blue-starred game ball on the turf twenty-three yards from the goal in the center of the field. Ten yards back, Liverpool lined up eight men in a wall to create a barrier. Anticipation grew as the fans knew that set plays like this were always dangerous opportunities for a team to score a goal. Would this one put Milan ahead at halftime? Would the Milan shooter go straight for

Kaká celebrates after beating Liverpool 2–1 to win the Champions League Final soccer match, May 23, 2007.

the goal, looking for a way around Liverpool's wall? Or would he pass to a teammate who could take a quick shot from another angle?

Milan's striker Filippo Inzaghi had lined up on the edge of Liverpool's wall. As soon as Pirlo struck the ball, he turned and sprinted toward the goal. The shot bent around the inside edge of the wall, curling toward the left side of the goal. Goalkeeper Reina dove to his left and looked like he would cover the shot. But as Inzaghi turned to look back, the ball struck him on the shoulder and deflected back toward the other side of the goal, behind Reina. Goal Milan!

The goal gave Milan momentum that they carried into the second half, pressing their attack as Liverpool's defense began to weaken. The score remained 1–0, however, until the final ten minutes.

In an effort to come from behind as the end of the game approached, Liverpool substituted in another attacker to try to come up with an equalizing goal. Liverpool's Mascherano went out, and Kaká quickly made the most of the opportunity. Shaking Mascherano's shadow, Kaká quickly found some freedom and space on the field. Right away he chipped a pass to Inzaghi in front of the open goal, but the striker couldn't get the shot on goal.

A few minutes later, Kaká received a pass and dribbled the ball with lots of open space toward Liverpool's goal box, shuffled subtly as if he might shoot, then sent a crisp through-ball between three defenders. Inzaghi rushed through from across the center and had only the goalie between him and the net. With one touch he pushed the ball toward the baseline to avoid the charging Reina. Then, from a difficult angle, he sent the ball rolling beneath the goalie's dive, across the goal mouth, and into the opposite side net. Goal!

Inzaghi ran to the corner and grabbed the corner flag. He fell to his knees pumping his fists and shouting, then lowered his face to the ground. Kaká was the first team-mate to run and embrace him. Milan had a 2–0 lead.

Liverpool attacked desperately and received a corner kick in the eighty-ninth minute. The ball sailed in to the near corner of the goal box. It was headed across the goal toward Dirk Kuyt near the far post, and Kuyt headed the ball into the back of the net to cut the lead in half.

Two years ago these very same teams had faced off in the 2005 Champions League final. A.C. Milan took a 3–0 lead into halftime, only to see Liverpool unbelievably fight back to send the game into a shootout tiebreaker, then win on penalty kicks. Could the Reds find another miracle comeback?

But time was on Milan's side in this game, and the referee blew his final whistle three minutes later. The Rossoneri were the champions of Europe and arguably of the whole world.

The Italian fans went wild, and Liverpool fans cried. Kaká and his teammates celebrated joyously, and fans cheered and sang in the stands as confetti rained onto the field. Kaká stripped off his jersey to reveal a white t-shirt with big black lettering that said "I belong to Jesus" in English. The Brazilian star ran a victory lap around the field cheering and waving both arms to the fans as a cluster of cameramen and photographers tried to keep up. Finally, Milan was presented with the huge silver cup.

The victory completed an amazing year for Kaká, but there were even more accolades to come. Many sports magazines had been calling Kaká the best player in the world. In October he was officially named the Federation Internationale des Associations de Footballers Professionels (FIFPro) 2007 World Player of the Year, voted on by more than forty-five thousand soccer professionals around the world.

In December he received the prestigious Ballon d'Or, or Golden Ball, for the best player in world by France Football magazine. And later that month, Kaká was voted the FIFA World Player of the Year by the world's national team coaches and captains.

"It's really special for me — it was a dream for me just to play for São Paulo and one game for Brazil," Kaká said when he accepted the golden trophy. "But the Bible says God can give you more than you even ask for and that is what has happened in my life."

Kaká had been dreaming big since he was a boy, and his faith had carried him even when the odds seemed long that he would ever become a soccer player. But with hard work, determination, and humility he had reached great heights. This is the story of how it all happened.

Toward the Goal: The Kaká Story

Jeremy V. Jones

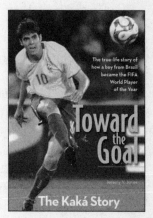

At the age of eight, Kaká already knew what he wanted in life: to play soccer and only soccer. He started playing in front of his friends and family, but when he suffered a crippling injury, doctors told him he would never play again. Through faith and perseverance Kaká recovered, and today he plays in front of thousands of fans every year. As the 2007 FIFA World Player of the Year and winner of the Ballon d'Or, this midfielder for Real Madrid has become one of the most recognized faces on the soccer field.

"I learned that it is faith that decides whether something will happen or not."

Available in stores and online!

Gifted Hands, Kids Edition:
The Ben Carson Story

Gregg Lewis & Deborah Shaw Lewis

Ben Carson used to be the class dummy. Today he is one of the world's most brilliant surgeons.

Gifted Hands, Kids Edition tells the extraordinary true story of an angry, young boy from the inner city who, through faith and determination, grew up to become one of the world's leading pediatric neurosurgeons. When Ben was in school, his peers called him the class dummy. But his mother encouraged him to succeed, and Ben discovered a deep love of learning. Ben found that anything is possible with trust and determination.

Available in stores and online!

Man on a Mission: The Tim Tebow Story

Jesse Florea

From Football Field to Mission Field

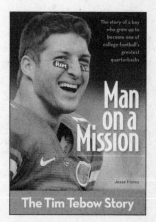

Tim Tebow is one of the greatest quarterbacks in college football history, a winner of the Heisman Trophy, a two-time recipient of the Maxwell Award, and a first-round draft pick for the Denver Broncos. But beyond the cheers and awards, Tim knows that the real glory goes to God. His conduct on the field and his tireless work in spreading the gospel through mission work have earned him a place in history. Learn the extraordinary true story of how the child who was never supposed to live inspired a nation.

Available in stores and online!

We want to hear from you. Please send your comments about this book to us in care of zreview@zondervan.com. Thank you.